People of the Bible

The Bible through stories and pictures

Adam and Eve

Copyright © in this format Belitha Press Ltd., 1983

Text copyright © Catherine Storr 1983

Illustrations copyright © Jim Russell 1983

Art Director: Treld Bicknell

First published in the United States of America 1983
by Raintree Publishers Limited Partnership
310 West Wisconsin Avenue, Milwaukee, Wisconsin 53203
in association with Belitha Press Ltd., London.

Conceived, designed and produced by Belitha Press Ltd.,
2 Beresford Terrace, London N5 2DH

ISBN 0-8172-1981-1 (U.S.A.)

Library of Congress Cataloging in Publication Data

Storr, Catherine.
  Adam and Eve.

   (People of the Bible)
   Summary: Retells the story of Adam and Eve's
temptation in the Garden of Eden and their subsequent,
ignominious departure.
   1. Adam (Biblical figure)—Juvenile literature, 2. Eve
(Biblical figure)—Juvenile literature. [I. Adam (Biblical
figure) 2. Eve (Biblical figure) 3. Bible stories—O.T.]
I. Russell, Jim, 1933- ill. II. Title.
BS580.A4S85   1983   222′.1109505   82-23060

ISBN 0-8172-1981-1

Printed in The United States of America.

   891011121314   97 96 95 94 93 92 91 90

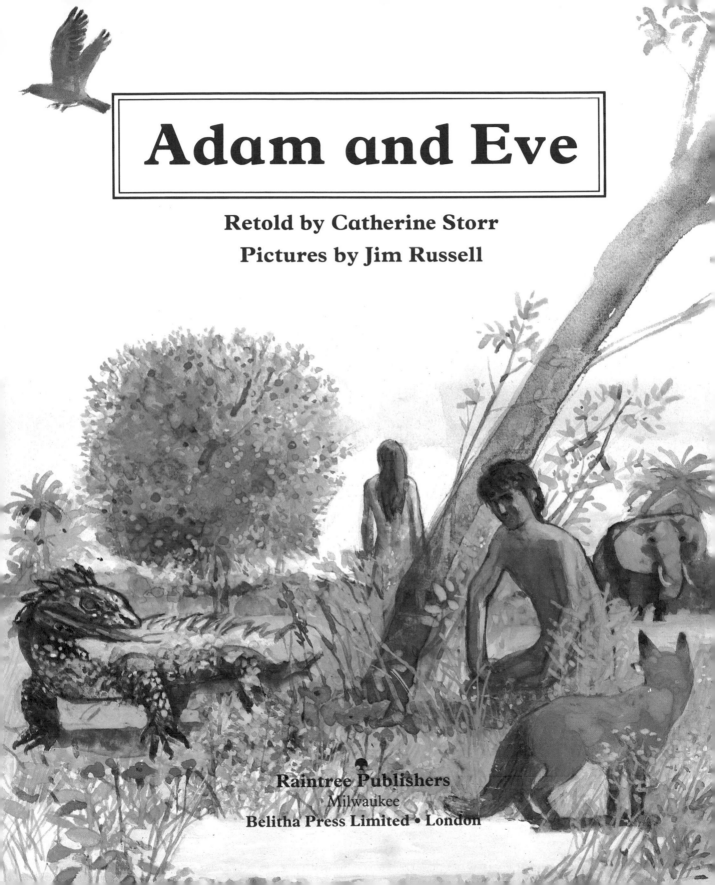

Adam and Eve

Retold by Catherine Storr
Pictures by Jim Russell

Raintree Publishers
Milwaukee
Belitha Press Limited • London

At the beginning of the world there was a man called Adam and a woman called Eve. They lived in the most beautiful garden you can imagine. It was called the garden of Eden. Every kind of tree and flower grew there, and every kind of animal lived there, too.

There were horses and giraffes, crocodiles and cows, monkeys and hares. There were sheep and dogs and goats and tigers.

There were leopards and kangaroos, hedgehogs and foxes, beetles, butterflies, frogs, and lizards. There were fish in the river and birds in the trees.

God said to Adam, "You can eat the fruit of all the trees here, except for the fruit of that special tree, the Tree of Knowledge. If you do, you will surely die."

Adam and Eve were very happy. God had told all the animals to do whatever Adam and Eve asked. They could understand everything the animals said, and the animals understood them and loved them.

But there was one animal in the garden who did not like to be told what to do. That was the serpent. "Why should Adam and Eve order me around?" he thought. One day the serpent searched the garden till he found Eve alone. She was making garlands of flowers for herself and Adam to wear on their heads as crowns.

"Beautiful woman, Eve, why do you
waste your time picking flowers?"

"Look at that tree with the big, golden apples hanging among the green leaves. Why don't you pick one of those apples and eat it?" the serpent asked.

"God told us not to eat the fruit from that tree," Eve said. "He says that if we eat it, we shall die."

The serpent laughed. "What nonsense! Your God wants to frighten you," he said.

"If you ate the fruit of this Tree of Knowledge, you would know as much as he does, and he wouldn't like that."

The serpent's narrow head and forked tongue pointed toward a beautiful apple hanging low from the Tree of Knowledge. "Go on!" he whispered. "Taste that apple, and see how wise you will become."

19

"I would like to know as much as God," Eve thought. She picked the apple and took a bite. It was delicious. She went off to find Adam. "Do taste this apple," she said. "It's wonderful." So Adam ate the rest of the apple.

The serpent laughed. "Now Adam and Eve will be punished. They won't be able to order me around any more."

When Adam and Eve had finished eating, they felt very uncomfortable. "We are different from all other animals who have fur and feathers," they said to each other. "We need to cover ourselves up. Let's make ourselves clothes out of leaves."

That evening, they saw God walking in the garden. They knew he would be angry with them, so they hid among the trees. But God called out, "Adam, where are you? Why are you hiding from me?"

"We didn't want to see you until we had some clothes to put on," Adam said.

Then God was angry. "Have you eaten the fruit of the Tree of Knowledge?" he asked.

Adam said, "Eve gave it to me, and I ate it."

"What have you done?" God said to Eve.

"The serpent beguiled me, and I ate," answered Eve.

God punished Adam and Eve.

"You must leave the garden of Eden," he
said. "And you will have to work hard for
your living, and grow your food yourself."
So Adam and Eve were sent away.

God was angry with the serpent, too. "From now on you and your children will have no legs and will eat dust," he said.

Ever since then, snakes have had to creep along the ground on their bellies.

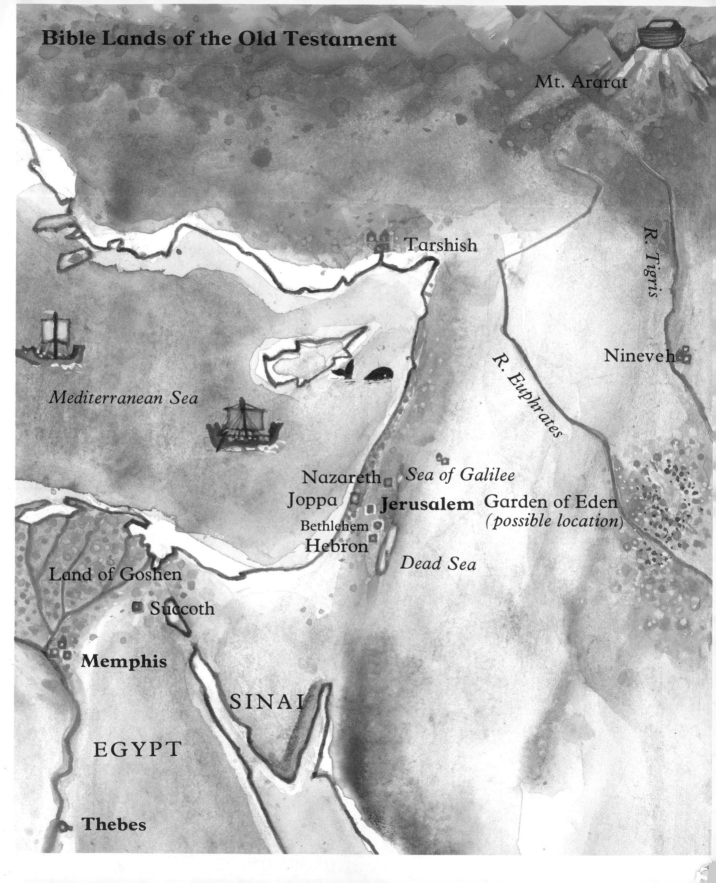

Bible Lands of the Old Testament

Mt. Ararat

R. Tigris

Tarshish

Nineveh

R. Euphrates

Mediterranean Sea

Sea of Galilee

Nazareth

Joppa **Jerusalem** Garden of Eden
(possible location)

Bethlehem

Hebron

Dead Sea

Land of Goshen

Succoth

Memphis

SINAI

EGYPT

Thebes